To the Full!

E   F

What People are Saying About
FULLY ALIVE

Jeff Kapusta is one of today's most outstanding communicators, and *Fully Alive* is a testament to that exceptional skill. With clarity, insight, and a rare ability to truly connect with his audience, Jeff has crafted a work that speaks to every believer who desires the abundant fullness that God has promised in every aspect of their lives. His teaching has profoundly impacted my own personal journey. Over the years, I've had the privilege of working alongside renowned authors and speakers like Dr. David Jeremiah, Ken Ham, the late Dr. Charles Stanley, and others. Yet, Jeff Kapusta has quickly become one of my all-time favorites. Whether you're seeking inspiration, practical advice, or a fresh perspective on all that God has for you, this book is a must-read.

—Ray Flynn
President and Chief Executive Officer,
Abraham Productions, Inc.
Founder of Sea Walker Media

My good friend Jeff has written a timely book for all of us who know there is more to life, but we aren't always sure what it is or how to experience it. This book is thoroughly biblical and incredibly practical, taking the lives of real people from the Bible and bringing their lives into the twenty-first century. As I read, it felt like he was walking alongside me like a tour guide on life's journey. I could not recommend this book with higher regard because I know from experience the man who wrote it is living out what he is writing and has led thousands on this same journey.

—Quovadis Marshall
Lead Pastor, Hope City Church

Fully Alive is filled with encouragement, wisdom, and practical tools to walk in the fullness of all God has for you. I've known Jeff for many years, and he lives what he teaches. *Fully Alive* is a great book for anyone who wants to overcome their past and live life to the fullest.

—Matt Fry
Lead Pastor, HopeFront Church

Jeff Kapusta is as real as they come. Over the past decade, I've watched him live out the abundant life he preaches with a deep love for Jesus and unshakable authenticity. Jeff doesn't just talk about purpose, joy, and faith—he lives it, day in and day out. *Fully Alive* reflects the passion and heart he brings to everything, and I know it'll inspire others to step into the fullness of life God has for them.

—Adam Magaña
Lead Pastor, Active Church
San Luis Obispo, CA

My friend Jeff has a track record of putting into practice the principles he preaches. In this book, you will find needed words to sustain important work. Many are emptied of life while pursuing success. *Fully Alive* unpacks bedrock keys for all who wish to experience life in themselves while extending it to others. If you're looking for applicable truths to keep you filled up as you pour out, then grab your copy today.

—Micah McElveen
CEO of Vapor Ministries
Author of *Dying for Purpose*

I love the genius of this book. Jeff Kapusta brilliantly approaches the quest for a life of meaning and purpose by laying out a practical map to become fully alive. Jeff has gifted you and me with a timely and helpful resource that helps us grasp not only the big picture of faith in Jesus but also how to walk that faith journey out. *Fully Alive* isn't just theory and ideas but a road map with accessible next steps. It's rare to find a book that is both enjoyable to read and full of practical applications. I'll be recommending this book far and wide!

—Marty Schmidt
Lead Pastor of The Bridge Church, IA

Fully Alive is a refreshing and timely reminder of the abundant life Jesus offers. My friend, Jeff Kapusta, weaves together wisdom, personal stories, and biblical insight to challenge us to live with purpose and joy, embracing all that God has for us. This book will inspire you to stop settling for less and step into the vibrant, fulfilling life that was always meant to be yours.

—Pastor Greg Surratt
Founding Pastor of Seacoast Church
Co-founder of the Association of Related Churches
Author

Jeff Kapusta is a true leader—his life exemplifies what it means to serve and love others wholeheartedly. His contagious passion for living with purpose inspires everyone around him. In this book, Jeff masterfully explores what it means to live a full and meaningful life, and I'm here for it! As someone who lives a busy, fast-paced life, at times, I find myself chasing the next thing. But Jeff beautifully reminds us that everything we need to live a purposeful and abundant life is already within our reach. I'm excited for this book to impact lives. I'm confident readers will discover rich purpose and practical wisdom within its pages. There's something here for everyone, and I'm deeply grateful for Jeff's insights and his willingness to share them with the world.

—Andy Williamson
Theory Communication & Design
Factory CLT

In *Fully Alive*, Jeff Kapusta extends a heartfelt invitation to embrace a life of more that only Jesus can offer. Through practical wisdom, engaging stories, and a fresh, relatable perspective, this book challenges readers to move beyond merely existing and step boldly into a life filled with purpose, joy, and authenticity. If you've ever felt like you're settling for a "half-full" life, *Fully Alive* offers a roadmap to a life over-flowing with God's best. This book is an inspiring call to live with intentionality and passion every day.

—Chris VanBuskirk
Lead Pastor, Centerpoint Church

Within the pages of this book, you will find a practical roadmap for living the full life God intended for you. Jeff takes you step by step, giving practical and attainable instructions whether you are new to the faith or have been following Jesus for many years. His insight will encourage you while also challenging you to become all that God has created you to be. I believe this book will be an investment into your personal growth that will produce fruit for years to come.

—Daniel Floyd
Senior Pastor, Lifepoint Church, Fredericksburg, VA

Jeff Kapusta is a friend and leader I deeply admire. What he has written in *Fully Alive* is more than just a book—it's a roadmap to the vibrant life God designed for us. With time-less truths and relatable insights, Jeff shows how to break free from past mistakes and step into a Spirit-filled, empow-ered life equipped for the journey ahead. Whether you're feeling stuck, searching for direction, or longing to grow in your faith, this book will inspire you to embrace God's best with confidence. A must-read for anyone ready to move from merely surviving to fully thriving!

—Justin Jenkins
Lead Pastor, Velocity Church

I've had the privilege of knowing Jeff Kapusta personally for years. I've witnessed firsthand the integrity of his char-acter, the depth of his faith, and his unwavering passion to see others thrive in their relationship with God. Fully Alive reflects the life Jeff lives—authentic, intentional, and rooted in the abundant life Jesus promised. He has a gift for taking deep biblical truths and making them both practical and inspiring. This book will challenge you to stop settling for less and equip you to step boldly into the fullness of life God created you for. Lean in because what you'll discover here could change your life.

—Nate Puccini
Chief of Staff, Substance Church

Pastor Jeff Kapusta is a leading voice in Christianity and leadership today. The more time I spend with him the more I realize how much better my life is because of him and how much he helps me grow my relationship with Jesus and others. *Fully Alive* is a book that practically discusses the why and the how of living your life fully alive in the power of Jesus! This book will help you not only understand what that looks like but also how to put it into action and work it every day of your life. Read this book and live it out—you will be grateful!

—Brandon Goff
Lead Pastor, Radiate Church

This is perhaps the most concise and helpful summary I've ever read of Christ's offer to give us life to the fullest. Every new believer in our church needs this, and it's a refreshingly simple backfill for older believers who've been living on empty. It's a practical field guide that every church needs on hand and in bulk. Jeff Kapusta doesn't waste words. He's brilliant, elegant, simple and fresh.

—Peter Haas
Author of *Broken Escalators*
Pastor of Substance Church

FULLY
ALIVE

For foreign and subsidiary rights, contact the author.

Cover design by Josh Tyndall
Cover photo by Josh Tyndall

ISBN: 978-1-962401-83-8   1 2 3 4 5 6 7 8 9 10

Printed in the United States of America

FULLY

God's will for everyone,
everywhere.

ALIVE

JEFF KAPUSTA

ARROWS & STONES

CONTENTS

INTRODUCTION

We've all been there. Anxiety mounting. Temperature climbing. Irritability at an all-time high.

People everywhere with no sense of urgency.

Red lights. Rush hour. Running late. Fuel light on. Gas gauge on empty.

I'll never forget running out of gas. One minute, everything was fine, and the next, my Jeep Cherokee started sputtering. My eyes looked down, and immediately, I knew.

I looked at my wife and said, "We're out of gas."

The car coasted to the side of the road where we sat and came up with a plan. Before we had time to call someone, a police officer pulled up behind us.

As he approached the car, he asked if we were having car trouble to which I said, "We're out of gas."

In the most sarcastic tone possible, he said, "If only our cars let us know when we're running low on gas, we would never end up in these situations."

I could smell what he was stepping in. He gave me a lift to the nearest gas station where I filled a can and brought it back to the Jeep. Thirty minutes and a bruised ego later, we were back on the road.

So much of life is lived this way.

Fuel level is low.

Two miles to empty.

God did not create you to run on fumes. As a matter of fact, Jesus said:

> *"The thief comes only to steal and kill
> and destroy; I have come that [you] may
> have life, and have it to the full."*
> —John 10:10

We'll come back to the first part of that verse in a moment. Right now, I want to draw your attention to "to the full." Jesus came so that we can live a full life.

The question must be asked, "If Jesus came so that we may have life to the full, why would we ever settle for anything less?"

Imagine pulling up to the gas pump and someone says to you, "Today is your lucky day. . . . You are customer #100 which means gas is on us today; how much would you like?"

You wouldn't ask for a quarter tank! You'd say, "Fill that sucker up!"

Or what if you ordered a dozen donuts and as you drive off, you realize they only put six in the box?

Or . . . Instacart delivers only half of your order?

What if . . . Papa John's delivered only half a pizza?

FULLY ALIVE

How about this? You order a large latte, and as you drive away, you realize it is less than half-full.

Here's my point: *If you wouldn't settle for a half-full latte, don't settle for a half-full life.*

Turn to your neighbor and say, "Never settle!"

In the second century, French Bishop Saint Irenaeus said, "The glory of God is man fully alive."[1]

You weren't meant to merely survive but to be fully alive.

The following eight chapters will walk you through the necessary components of a full life. You can certainly take this journey on your own, but I strongly encourage you to walk through it with others.

> *"If you want to go fast, go alone. If you want to go far, go together."*
> —African proverb

---

1   Saint Irenaeus of Lyons, *Against Heresies* (CreateSpace Independent Publishing Platform, March 28, 2012).

CHAPTER 1

FORGIVEN BY CHRIST

A quick Google search of the question, "What is my purpose?" yields about 5,790,000,000 potential links you can click.

I don't know about you, but I don't have that kind of time. If it's okay with you, we'll just go straight to the source.

God.

If you've ever wanted to know God's will for your life . . . you're in the right place.

God's will is found in God's Word.

While I can't tell you what your purpose is as it pertains to whether you should take this job or that, marry this woman or that woman, or live near the mountains or the beach, what I can tell you is that God's will for you is to live a life that is FULLY ALIVE.

I'll make you this promise: you live FULLY ALIVE, and the rest of life's questions will become clear.

FULLY ALIVE

Let's start with the most important aspect of a life FULLY ALIVE:

A LIFE FULLY ALIVE IS A LIFE FORGIVEN BY CHRIST.

Has anyone ever said to you, "I have good news and bad news? Which do you want first?" If you're like me, you want the bad news first, so you can end on a good note.

Here's the bad news: you, my friend, are a sinner.

I hate to be the bearer of bad news, but it's true.

The Bible says that "all have sinned and fallen short of the glory of God" (Romans 3:23).

Sin simply means "to miss the mark."

To sin is to fall short of all that God had in mind when He created you. It's the things we do that we shouldn't do, and it's the things we should do but don't do.

We read about sin entering the world in the book of Genesis when Adam and Eve chose to disobey God's instructions. As a result, sin entered our world. It destroys everything it touches— the worst of which is our relationship with our heavenly Father.

Sin has infected and affected every generation.

In the introduction of this book, I said that we'd come back to the first part of John 10:10: "The thief comes only to steal, kill and destroy."

There is an enemy in this world that wants nothing more than to disrupt the plans of God and destroy the good that He has for you.

Let's just be honest, most of our current headlines are a reminder that there is a thief who is really good at his job.

He destroys relationships, introduces us to addictions and unhealthy behaviors, attacks our identity, and even goes as far as to tell us that the world wouldn't miss us if we weren't here. He's a thief, a murderer, and a liar.

"Therefore, just as sin entered the world through one man, and death through sin, and in this way death came to all people, because all sinned."
—Romans 5:12

That's the bad news. Sin→Death.

Thank God there is good news.

"For just as through the disobedience of the one man the many were made sinners, so also through the obedience of the one man the many will be made righteous."
—Romans 5:19

What this means is that in the same way, the consequences of sin have impacted everyone, but so has the sacrifice of Jesus. He is the "one Man."

Just because a gift is given does not mean it has been received.

This is great news! Regardless of your past, God has a future for you:

> *There is no difference between Jew and Gentile, for all have sinned and fall short of the glory of God, and all are* justified *freely by his grace through the redemption that came by Christ Jesus. God presented Christ as a sacrifice of atonement, through the shedding of his blood—to be received by faith. —Romans 3:22-25 (author emphasis added)*

The Greek word for "justified" is *dikaioō*: "to cause someone to be in a proper or right relationship with someone else."

Just because a gift is given does not mean it has been received.

The reason the sacrifice of Jesus is such a big deal is that only a perfect, unblemished sacrifice could offer forgiveness for sin. Jesus did that.

But . . .

Just because a gift is given does not mean that it has been received.

Verse 24 says that we "are justified freely by his grace." Grace is a gift that must be received.

We are FORGIVEN BY CHRIST when we acknowledge and repent of our sins and make Jesus the Lord and Savior of our lives.

If you've never made this decision, you can do it right now. Pray this prayer:

Dear Jesus, thank You for loving me. I know I don't deserve it, but today, I choose to receive it. I repent of my sin, and I turn my

*life over to You. I ask You to forgive me,
change me, and fill me with Your Holy Spirit.
Thank You for the gift of grace. Help me live
for You so that I can be fully alive. Amen.*

If you just prayed that prayer, I want to be the first to say, "Congratulations!" What you made was a very private decision. Now, I want to encourage you to tell a friend and make it public with baptism.

NEXT STEPS:

» Tell somebody. Phone a friend. Tell your parents. Tell a coworker. Tell a stranger. Just tell somebody.
» Get baptized. In the Bible, baptism typically happens immediately after someone puts their faith in Jesus. It is a symbolic way of saying, "I'm not who I used to be." I'm not perfect, but I am forgiven. I want the world to know that Jesus is my Savior. The only prerequisite for baptism is salvation. If you've said "yes" to Jesus, you are ready to say "yes" to baptism.

Talk it Over. Live it Out.

"Therefore, just as sin entered the world through one man, and death through sin, and in this way death came to all people, because all sinned. . . ."
—Romans 5:12

---

1) Have you struggled to accept grace or forgiveness, either from God or others? What seems to stand in your way? What helps you receive it?
2) What is the meaning of the verse above in your own words?
3) How has sin impacted your life? How did you seek restoration?
4) Have you accepted Christ? Have you told someone and been baptized?
5) If you have taken the above steps, how did they impact your faith journey? If not, what might be holding you back?

A LIFE FULLY ALIVE
IS A LIFE FORGIVEN
BY CHRIST.

CHAPTER 2

FOCUSED ON SCRIPTURE

"The thief comes only to steal and kill and destroy; I have come that they may have life, and have it to the full."
—John 10:10

J ust to be clear, when we say "Scripture," we are referring to the Bible which is the Word of God.

A life fully alive is focused on Scripture.
All of my life, I have had really good eyesight. Around the age of forty, I started noticing that my eyes were not as good as they used to be.

I was creeping closer to my computer and holding restaurant menus farther from my face.

I recently got my eyes checked and walked out with a prescription for progressive lenses. They help me with reading and allow me to see far away. They're essentially bifocals but without the noticeable line on the lens. When I got the call to pick up my new glasses, I was blown away when I put them on my face.

It's like my world went from standard def to 4k. Everything looked so crisp. It was as if the world came into focus.

God's Word is like that. It is a lens that brings life into focus.

THE WILL OF GOD WILL COME INTO FOCUS WHEN THE WORD OF GOD BECOMES OUR FOCUS.

The Bible is unlike any other collection of writings. It is alive. It is active. It is inspired by God. When you get into the Bible, the Bible begins to get into you.

Psalm 119:105 says, "Your word is a lamp for my feet, a light on my path."

The Word of God is like a lamp . . . not a flood light. It will illuminate your current surroundings and most likely your next step.

As you read the Bible you are, in essence, turning on the light. One of the best ways to discover God's plan for your life is to get into His Word.

WE KNOW THE WILL OF GOD BY READING THE WORD OF GOD.

Not only do I want you to get in the Word, but I also want you to have confidence that it is God's Word. If I were to ask you, "Do you trust that the Bible is true?" what would you say?

Most people would agree. But if I were to follow up with the question, "Why do you trust that the Bible is true?" most would respond with "Because the Bible says so."

Saying, "The Bible is trustworthy because the Bible says it's trustworthy," is called a circular argument.

Let me share with you a few cool insights about the Bible.

1) The Bible is not a book but a library.

I know it looks like a book. It's bound like a book, but it's more than a book. It is actually sixty-six books bound together in a collection.

2) God inspired the writing of the Bible.

Over thirty different authors, under the inspiration of the Holy Spirit, contributed to the writing of the Bible. Second Timothy 3:16 says that "all Scripture is God-breathed" . . . pretty cool thought. Want to know something else interesting? The writers came from very diverse backgrounds.

> » Moses wrote in the wilderness.
> » Jeremiah wrote in a dungeon.
> » Daniel wrote while exiled in Babylon.
> » David wrote in the pasture.
> » Solomon wrote in a palace.
> » Paul wrote in a prison.

3) The Bible was written over a period of 1,500 years.

From Genesis to Revelation, the writers span 1,500 years. This is important to know because some people will try to say, "How do we know a bunch of guys got together and collaborated on the Bible?" I think we'd all agree that a 1,500-year collaboration is pretty impressive. But come to think of it, I guess they did collaborate under the inspiration of the Holy Spirit.

4) The Bible was written in three languages on three continents.

The Bible was originally written in Hebrew, Aramaic, and Greek across the continents of Asia, Africa, and Europe.

Can we agree that anything written over a period of 1,500 years, in three languages, on three continents, by over thirty different people is pretty impressive?

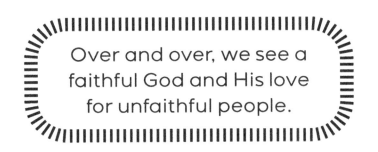

Over and over, we see a faithful God and His love for unfaithful people.

But wait . . . there's more.

5) The Bible has one central message.

What is the chance that the Bible would have continuity over a 1,500-year period?

Over and over, we see a faithful God and His love for unfaithful people.

The Bible is a reminder that God loves His children.

GOD LOVES YOU.

"The New Testament is 99.5% textually pure. In the entire text of 20,000 lines, only 40 lines are in question (about 400 words), and none affects any significant doctrine."[2]
—Norman Geisler, Historian

"To be skeptical of the resultant text of the New Testament books is to allow all of classical

---

2   "A Note on the Percent of Accuracy of the New Testament Text," *Norman Geisler*, normangeisler. com/a-note-on-the-percent-of-accuracy-of-the-new-testament-text/.

antiquity to slip into obscurity, for no documents of the ancient period are as well attested bibliographically as the New Testament."[3]
—John Warwick Montgomery

"Archaeologists have consistently discovered the names of government officials, kings, cities, and festivals mentioned in the Bible—sometimes when historians didn't think such people or places existed . . . not one archaeological find has conflicted with what the Bible records."[4]
—Nelson Glueck cited in *The Case for Christ*

"A thousand times over, the death knell of the Bible has been sounded, the funeral procession formed, the inscription cut on the tombstone, and committal read. But somehow the corpse never stays put. No other book has been so chopped, knifed, sifted, scrutinized, and vilified. What book on

---

3   John Warwick Montgomery, *History and Christianity* (Bethany House Pub, January 1, 1986).
4   Nelson Glueck, cited in Lee Strobel, *The Case for Christ* (Grand Rapids, MI: Zondervan Publishing House, 1998), 132.

philosophy or religion or psychology has been subject to such a mass attack as the Bible?"[5]
—Bernard Ramm

How you get in the Bible is not as important as what you get out of the Bible.

6) Can the Bible be trusted?

Yes! However, it doesn't matter that you trust the Bible if you're not getting in it and don't know how to use it!

The apostle Paul said that the Word of God is like a sword (see Hebrews 4:12). What is a sword? It is a weapon. Like any weapon, it is unwise to carry it without knowing how to use it.

---

5   Bernard Ramm, *Protestant Christian Evidences* (Chicago, IL: Moody Press, January 1, 1954).

Let's keep something important about reading the Bible in mind: *How you get in the Bible is not as important as what you get out of the Bible.*

For instance, it doesn't matter if you read a paper Bible or a digital one. It doesn't matter if you read in the morning or at night. It doesn't matter if you read from the Old Testament or the New Testament.

What does matter is that you read a translation you understand. The Bible was never a collection for the educated but for the ordinary.

Might I make a suggestion?

When you get some time, check out Bible.com and look for a seven-day reading plan.

- » Start with the Gospel of John.
- » Set a reminder on your phone.
- » Don't feel rushed.
- » If you miss a day, don't sweat it.
- » Write down or highlight what verses stand out to you.

You will find that certain verses will stand out for a reason.

WHAT YOU READ TODAY YOU'LL NEED TOMORROW, SO WRITE IT DOWN.

One great way to read and process the Bible is called the S.O.A.P. method. Here's how it works.

While you're reading the Bible, pay attention to what verses resonate with you and write your thoughts down in a journal as you follow the S.O.A.P. acronym.

S—Scripture: Write out the verse that stands out to you.
O—Observation: What is happening in this verse?
A—Application: How can you apply this verse?
P—Prayer: Write out your prayer to God.

Give it a try.

Hebrews 4:12-16:

> *For the word of God is alive and active. Sharper than any double-edged sword, it penetrates even to dividing soul and spirit, joints and marrow; it judges the thoughts and attitudes of the heart. Nothing in all creation is hidden from God's sight. Everything is uncovered and laid bare before the eyes of him to whom we must give account.*
>
> *Therefore, since we have a great high priest who has ascended into heaven, Jesus the Son of God, let us hold firmly to the faith we profess. For we do not have a high priest who is unable to empathize with our weaknesses, but we have one who has been tempted in every way, just as we are—yet he did not sin. Let us then approach God's throne of grace with confidence, so that we may receive mercy and find grace to help us in our time of need.*

FULLY ALIVE

S—_____
_____
_____
_____
_____

O—_____
_____
_____
_____
_____
_____

A—_____
_____
_____
_____
_____

P—_____
_____
_____
_____
_____
_____

A life FULLY ALIVE is a life focused on Scripture.

Talk it Over. Live it Out.

"For the word of God is alive and active. Sharper than any double-edged sword, it penetrates even to dividing soul and spirit, joints and marrow; it judges the thoughts and attitudes of the heart. Nothing in all creation is hidden from God's sight. Everything is uncovered and laid bare before the eyes of him to whom we must give account."

—Hebrews 4:12-13

---

1) What is the significance of comparing God's Word to a weapon?
2) Which method of Bible study do you find most effective for you, and why? How has it deepened your understanding of Scripture?
3) What are you facing in your life now that God's Word may be able to help you with?
4) Can you think of a time when reading the Bible helped you see a situation in your life more clearly? How did the Biblical perspective impact your actions or decisions?
5) How has your understanding of God's plan for your life evolved as you've spent more time reading the Bible?

A LIFE FULLY ALIVE IS FOCUSED ON SCRIPTURE.

CHAPTER 3

FREED FROM MY PAST

The thing about the past is that we all have one. Some good. Some not so much. Forgive me for prying, but can I ask what emotions emerge when you think about your past?

For some, your past emotes feelings of joy. You're thinking about your childhood, friends, family, holidays, and summers at the beach.

If you have a pulse,
you have a past.

For others, just thinking about the past is a reminder of the good ole days. You remember a season when you were on top of your game, life was good, but something happened. You tried your best to hold on to a season that was slipping away. You can't help but feel like your best days are behind you.

Then, some don't even want to think about it. Your past was painful. You said you'd never go back there. It's a reminder of what was and no longer is.

A relationship that didn't last. A career cut short. The loss of a loved one. The pain is real.

If you have a pulse, you have a past.

Can we talk about getting past the pain of your past?

"What's that? I'd rather not. It's in the past," you say.

Is it, though?

If your past is messing with your present, it's not in the past.

Too many well-meaning people are dragging their past through their present pretending it's not there.

You will never pretend your past away. It's time we talk about it.

There is life past the pain.

In the Old Testament book of Isaiah, God spoke a word to His people that it was time to move beyond their past.

It was time to leave the past and move into the promise:

> *Forget the former things; do not dwell on the past. See, I am doing a new thing! Now it springs up; do you not perceive it? I am making a way in the wilderness and streams in the wasteland.*
> *—Isaiah 43:18-19*

You will never see the "new thing" God has ahead of you as long as you keep dwelling on the "former things" behind you.

It's been said that your past is like the rearview mirror of a car. It's helpful to glance at what is behind, but staring at it won't make you arrive at your destination.

God asked His people, "Do you not perceive it?" In other words, God says, "You can't see the promise if you keep dwelling on your past."

Forget the former things.

FUHGEDDABOUDIT

(Said in my best Tony Soprano voice.)

Have you ever had someone tell you to "Just forget about it"? How in the world are you supposed to do that?

I'm not gonna try to tell you that it is easy, but I will tell you it is possible. I believe that if God is bringing your past into your present, it is because He wants to bring healing to it.

I've got a six-inch scar on my left shin from years ago. Here's what happened.

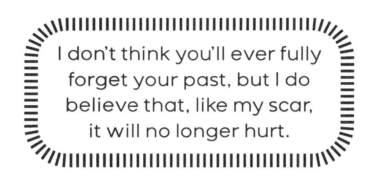

I don't think you'll ever fully forget your past, but I do believe that, like my scar, it will no longer hurt.

Our workout included thirty-inch box jumps one day at the gym. Fatigued, I jumped twenty-nine inches to a thirty-inch box.

Yup, you guessed it—my shin ate the box. It was awful. Bled for days.

Am I being a bit dramatic? Yes, a little.

My point is that while that incident happened years ago, the scar still remains. It reminds me of what happened, but it also reminds me that once a wound heals it no longer hurts.

I don't think you'll ever fully forget your past, but I do believe that, like my scar, it will no longer hurt.

Healing is in your future. Freedom is in your future. Perceive it.

Are you ready?

The first thing you must do is turn around and FACE IT.

Stop running from it.

You cannot outrun your past.

You must confront it.

Face It

It is all too common for people to move to a new city in pursuit of a new life full of new relationships, new hopes, and new dreams only to realize that they brought the same old, undealt past with them.

Let's talk about Moses for a minute.

Moses is the guy in the Old Testament book of Exodus who led millions of Hebrew people from oppression in Egypt toward the Promised Land.

Did you know that Moses had a past?

Moses:
  » Was threatened at birth.
  » Was given up by his parents.
  » Was rescued by Egyptians.
  » Grew up with wealth.
  » Knew he didn't fit in.
  » Got in a fight, killed a man, and buried the body.

Yes, you read that correctly.

When word began to spread about what he had done, he was terrified.

> *The next day, when Moses went out to visit his people again, he saw two Hebrew men fighting. "Why are you beating up your friend?" Moses said to the one who had started the fight. The*

man replied, "Who appointed you to be our prince and judge? Are you going to kill me as you killed that Egyptian yesterday?" Then Moses was afraid, thinking, "Everyone knows what I did."
—Exodus 2:13-14 (NLT, author emphasis added)

Read that last sentence again: "Everyone knows what I did."

I know what you did last summer. . . .

But running from your past won't make it go away. Let's make the decision today to stop running, turn around, and face it.

When you face the past, you can find forgiveness and freedom from it.

What do you need to face right now?

Don't worry, we won't stay here long, but we will start here.

The second part of the freedom process is to ADMIT IT.

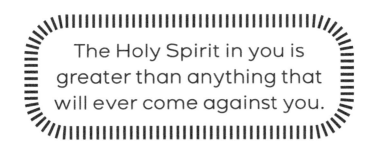

The Holy Spirit in you is greater than anything that will ever come against you.

Admit It

Admit that IT happened. Admit that what you did was wrong. Or maybe, what they did was wrong. Someone else's IT may be impacting many of us. The wake of their decisions is rippling through our lives.

Parents that couldn't work it out.

A spouse who wasn't faithful.

A friend who betrayed your trust.

An addiction in your family.

A boss who was dishonest.

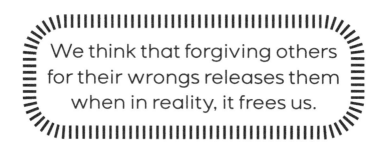
We think that forgiving others for their wrongs releases them when in reality, it frees us.

Unpopular opinion: stop waiting for someone else to apologize to you for what they did. You forgive them. Even if they haven't asked for forgiveness. Even if they never ask for forgiveness. You forgive them.

Forgiveness is the key that sets you free.

We think that forgiving others for their wrongs releases them when in reality, it frees us.

Let's be honest, they are out living their life. They aren't thinking about us. They have probably even moved on, but we are stuck.

We keep thinking about it. We are the ones plotting revenge.

Stop it.

Admit it.

Forgive it.

Don't let what THEY did steal another day of your life. Forgive them and take one more step toward your freedom.

Maybe the person you are struggling to forgive is the one staring back at you in the mirror.

You know what you did. You know the pain you caused. You know the shame you carry. You don't feel worthy of forgiveness. You believe that forgiveness is for everyone except you.

FULLY ALIVE

You've even allowed the failure of your past to sabotage your future. You tell yourself that you don't deserve to be happy, to be loved, or to be forgiven.

I know that you know this, but it bears repeating: nobody is perfect.

Good news, though—God can do great things through imperfect people.

Admit your sin, and acknowledge the pain.

For Moses, his past didn't disqualify him from his purpose. God didn't give up on him, and He hasn't given up on you.

> *"For all have sinned and fall*
> *short of the glory of God."*
> —Romans 3:23

I know we talked about this already, but I want to circle back for a second. All have sinned. Sin is real. Sin has consequences. Sin causes pain, but God brings healing.

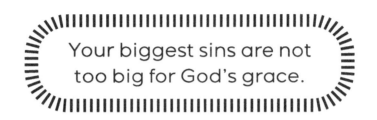

Your biggest sins are not
too big for God's grace.

Admitting that we have sinned is a critical part of the healing process.

Is there something in your past that you have been unwilling to admit? Can we deal with it now?

Your biggest sins are not too big for God's grace.

FACE IT.

ADMIT IT.

The third step to freedom is to REPLACE IT. Replace your past with God's future.

Replace It
God invites us to give Him our past in exchange for a new future. A good future. A hope-filled future.

FULLY ALIVE

God doesn't want to simply repair our past; He wants to replace it.

You are not what you have done. You are who God says you are.

Moses the murderer ran for his life. He ditched the palace for a pasture.

Fear of what he had done drove him away from all he had known.

In Exodus 3, we find Moses tending sheep on the backside of the wilderness. Little did Moses know that while he was running from his past, God was running after him.

One crazy conversation over a burning bush and several excuses later, Moses receives a new lease on life. Moses trades his failed past for a promising future.

You can't change your past, but God can change your future.

FACE IT→ADMIT IT→REPLACE IT

God is inviting you to trade in your past for His future. I know, I know—it sounds too good to be true.

You're right. I agree with you. It's the best deal going. But it's real.

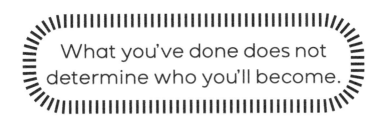

What you've done does not determine who you'll become.

Are you ready to face your past and replace it with God's future?

"Therefore, there is now no condemnation for those who are in Christ Jesus, because through Christ Jesus the law of the Spirit who gives life has set you free from the law of sin and death."
—Romans 8:1-2

FULLY ALIVE

*"If we confess our sins, he is faithful
and just and will forgive us our sins and
purify us from all unrighteousness."*
—1 John 1:9

Many years ago, I met a guy who told me he had ruined everything. He had a great marriage, a family, and a ministry until he lost it all.

He failed morally, and that failure uprooted everything in his life. He ran from God. He ran to self-destructive behaviors.

One day, he walked into church and heard a message about forgiveness. After the message, he approached me and said, "I have forgiven everyone except myself. I just can't."

I remember looking at him and saying, "How dare you withhold forgiveness from someone that God has already forgiven?"

I don't know where it came from, but I know it is what he needed to hear. Maybe it's what you need to hear also. God loves you. He has forgiven you. Receive it.

What you've done does not determine who you'll become.

Be free.

Talk it Over. Live it Out.

"Therefore, there is now no condemnation for those who are in Christ Jesus, because through Christ Jesus the law of the Spirit who gives life has set you free from the law of sin and death."
—Romans 8:1-2

---

1) Have you struggled to accept God's forgiveness for something in your past?
2) How do feelings about your past influence your current mindset and actions?
3) How does the verse above affect the way you view your past?
4) Reflect on someone you need to forgive, including yourself. What barriers are preventing you from offering or receiving forgiveness? How can you overcome them?
5) What specific steps can you take, or have you taken, to replace your past with the future God has planned for you? How can embracing this new future change your outlook and actions?

IF YOUR PAST IS MESSING WITH YOUR PRESENT, IT'S NOT IN THE PAST.

CHAPTER 4

FOUND IN FAMILY

" **W**e are family. All my brothers, sisters, and me."[6]

How you read that lyric in your head exposes a thing or two about your age.

If you read it like any ordinary sentence, you are in the younger demographic.

But if you read it and automatically chopped up the word "family" into fam-mil-ly, you're probably getting mail from AARP.

Have you ever noticed at church how people tend to refer to each other as "brother" or "sister"? Someone approaches you and asks, "How are you, brother?"

You probably thought it was because they couldn't remember your name, and you would be correct.

But there's another reason church people like to refer to other church people as "brother" and "sister."

---

6   Sister Sledge, vocalists, "We Are Family," by Bernard Edwards and Nile Rodgers, released April 1979, track 5 on *We Are Family*, Cotillion.

Church is a family.

In the Bible, there are several metaphors for the church but the most popular one is that of family.

In the New Testament book of Ephesians, the apostle Paul wrote:

Through [Jesus] we both have access to the Father by one Spirit. Consequently, you are no longer foreigners and strangers, but fellow citizens with God's people and also members of his household. —Ephesians 2:18-19

There are several heavy-hitting truths tucked in these two verses.

1) Jesus grants us access to the Father.
2) God is our Father.
3) We are no longer outsiders but insiders.
4) We are no longer strangers but family members.

Family has access.

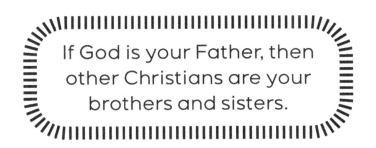

If God is your Father, then other Christians are your brothers and sisters.

Remember when you were a kid and went to a friend's house? Some rooms were just off-limits to you. You didn't go to the dining room, office, or parents' room.

The living room was fine. The kitchen was fine. Your friend's room was fine. But some rooms . . . not fine.

Why?

Because you were a guest. It was not your family's house.

However, when you are at your house you have no problem barging into any room you please. It is for this reason that your parents put locks on the doors!

When you put your faith in Jesus you have access to your heavenly Father's house. If God is your Father, then other Christians are your brothers and sisters.

We are family. (You sounded it out again, didn't you?)

This is the mental picture I want you to have.

The church is not a building.

The church is not an event.

The church is not a club.

The church is a FAMILY.

The church is not so much something you "go to" but something you are a "part of."

If you are new to church, let me be one of the first to say, "WELCOME TO THE FAMILY!"

I know that not everyone reading this has a good mental picture of family.

Some of us come from great families. Your memory is full of family outings, holidays, vacations, weekends, sporting events, and birthday parties.

For others, your mental picture of family is broken. For that, I am sorry. Our earthly family is supposed to be a reflection of our heavenly family. Sadly, for many, the mirror has been shattered, and the reflection is broken.

When God created you, He created you for family.

"Let us do good to all people, especially to those who belong to the family of believers."
—Galatians 6:10

The church is family caring for family.

YOU WERE MADE FOR FAMILY

When it comes to God, family is a big deal. Hebrews 2:11 says, "Both the one who makes people holy and those who are made holy are of the same family.

So Jesus is not ashamed to call them brothers and sisters." How awesome is this!?!?

Not only is Jesus the One who makes us holy, but He is also not ashamed to call us His brothers and sisters.

Jesus is not ashamed of you!

Go back and read that again.

Jesus has called you to be part of His family. This is a good thing.

Have you ever heard the saying, "You mess with me, you mess with my whole family"?

When Jesus is your Brother and God is your Father, this saying takes on a whole new meaning. How about this one, "My dad can beat up your dad."

As a family, we are better together. Can I ask a question? "Who makes you better?" Let me ask it another way. "Who is better because of you?" Remember that African proverb from the introduction?

> *"If you want to go fast, go alone.*
> *If you want to go far, go together."*

We are better together.

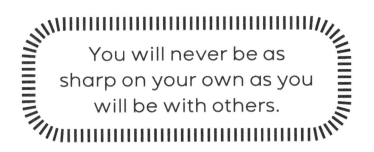

You will never be as sharp on your own as you will be with others.

Getting around others is one of the best ways to grow in your knowledge of God, the Bible, and church stuff. Many churches offer small groups, connect groups, home groups, e-groups, or some other randomly named groups.

Bottom line is that we need to be around others who will encourage us and challenge us.

Proverbs 27:17 says, "As iron sharpens iron, so one person sharpens another." You will never be as sharp on your own as you will be with others.

Technically, according to this verse, your life would be dull without others in your life.

Tired of being dull? Try a group (poorly worded small group promotion!)

In a Family, You Belong

The great thing about family is that all you have to do to belong is show up. My kids instantly became part of the family the day they were born.

As a matter of fact, we started creating a place for them before they ever got here. They had their own room. Fully decorated. Fully stocked. It came with a twenty-four-hour butler, maid, and surveillance services. The only thing required of my kids was to show up!

When I started dating my wife and she took me to meet her family, they didn't make me sit in another room while they had family dinner. How weird would that have been? They invited me in and had a seat and a plate ready just for me.

All I did was show up.

When it comes to the church family, you need to know that you belong. There is a place for you.

Last time I checked, the church doesn't hang a KEEP OUT sign on the front door.

The more I think about it, the church is one of the few organizations that exists for its non-members. Whether you are new on your faith journey or still kicking the tires, you need to know that you belong.

You Don't Have to Clean Up to Show Up

This doesn't even make sense to me. Maybe you've heard people say that they can't go to church until they get some stuff in their lives straightened out.

I can't go to the gym until I lose some weight.

I can't go to the doctor because I'm sick.

I can't go to the dentist because my teeth are nasty.

If you will show up, God will do the cleaning.

If you have to clean up in order to show up, none of us would be here.

Just. Show. Up.

Regardless of your background, you belong.

Didn't grow up in church? That's okay.

Don't know the Bible? That's okay.

Regardless of your baggage, you belong.

Got a past? Welcome to the club.

Regardless of your bank account, you belong.

Your net worth does not determine your self-worth.

Regardless of your behavior, you belong.

Every family has some crazy in it. That's okay.

Regardless of your brokenness, you belong.

> *"There's a million ways to be broken*
> *and one way to be made whole."*
> —Source Unknown

In Luke 15, Jesus was telling stories to help people understand what the heart of the Father is like.

One of His stories was about a father with two sons. In that culture, it was understood that a father would leave an inheritance to his boys upon his death.

The younger son got it in his head that the life he really wanted was out on his own, away from his father. So, this boy approached his dad and demanded his share of the inheritance early so that he could go off and live his life.

The inheritance was always going to be his if he had just been patient.

To the surprise of the audience, the father gave his son his inheritance and let him leave.

The boy went off, lived it up, and chased his dreams. Unfortunately, his dreams turned into nightmares, and he fell hard.

Rock bottom hard.

Verse 17 says that "when he came to his senses," he realized that the servants in his father's house were living better than he was. He messed up big time. He swallowed his pride and began the long journey home.

His father saw him coming up the driveway.

I imagine from a distance they locked eyes.

Dad starts running. Why is he running? Is he running to me or at me? As the dad reached his son he threw his arms around him.

He hugged him. He restored him.

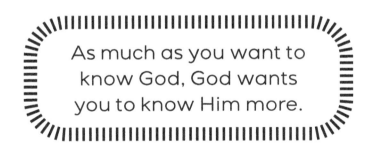

As much as you want to know God, God wants you to know Him more.

It's a beautiful story. You really need to read it.

FULLY ALIVE

All the son did was show up. When he showed up, Dad showed off.

Dad restored him and then threw him a party! A welcome home party!

Keep showing up. If you don't believe all this Jesus stuff yet, that's okay. Keep showing up.

As much as you want to know God, God wants you to know Him more.

Talk it Over. Live it Out.

"Therefore, as we have opportunity, let us do good to all people, especially to those who belong to the family of believers."
—Galatians 6:10

---

1) In what practical ways can you contribute to and benefit from being part of a church family?
2) No one has to "clean up" before coming to church. How can embracing this truth change your approach to participating in church and community?
3) Share a personal experience where you felt the church acted as a family for you. What impact did this experience have on your faith and sense of community?
4) How does knowing you have access to God's family impact your sense of belonging and your interactions with other believers?
5) If your experience with family has been difficult, how can viewing the church as a family help you find healing and a sense of belonging?

IF GOD IS YOUR FATHER, THEN OTHER CHRISTIANS ARE YOUR BROTHERS AND SISTERS.

CHAPTER 5

FATHERED BY GOD

I t was the final inning of the game. My team was down by two and up to bat. We had two outs.

I was up to bat.

The count was three balls and two strikes.

I had never hit a ball over the fence . . . ever. Until then.

The pitch was perfect. I swung with everything I had. Solid contact. I ran with everything I had.

As I rounded first, my coach, who also was my dad, sent me to second and shouted, "It's over the fence; it's over the fence!"

I had never heard those words before.

It was a rare occasion that he would send someone with my speed past first base and on toward second.

Why did he do that? What is "over the fence"?

FULLY ALIVE

It didn't make sense. He knew something I didn't, so I chugged along to second where it began to register that I had just hit the game-winning, walk-off home run!

What just happened?

My team met me at the plate and celebrated me more than I had ever been celebrated. It was epic. I was given the game ball that day.

As I think back over that day, I still feel the emotion of uncertainty I felt as I went to bat. I still feel the nerves, afraid that if I struck out, the game would be over.

But the biggest memory I have is of my dad, the first base coach, jumping, shouting, and waving me on for my home run trot. He was beaming.

So, tell me about your dad. What was he like?

Did he have any hobbies? In what ways are you like him? Did he have a smell?

I know it's a weird question, but my dad had a smell growing up. Brut aftershave.

Our dads have impacted all of us.

Present or absent.

According to statistics, "fatherlessness" is the greatest pandemic of our generation.[7] Every societal downfall can be traced back to the breakdown of the family and the absence of fathers.

According to Fatherhood.com, "A father's absence affects children in numerous unfortunate ways,

---

7   Kris Vallotton, *Uprising: The Epic Battle for the Most Fatherless Generation in History* (Minneapolis, MN: Chosen Books, 2022).

while a father's presence makes a positive difference in the lives of both children and mothers."[8]

DADDY ISSUES

Because of the absence of fathers, many in our generation are growing up with "father wounds" or "Daddy Issues." We can deny it, but the truth remains that an absent or abusive father causes deep issues of identity, affection, and affirmation.

In first-century Jewish culture, your father would've determined your inheritance. His name, property, and place in society determined your identity. You carried his name.

In the absence of a godly father, we develop a skewed view of our identity and our inheritance.

My counselor, Chip Judd, once said, "Whoever's words define you is your god."

---

8   "Father Absence Statistics," *National Fatherhood Initiative*, www.fatherhood.org/father-absence-statistic.

Hang with me. He tells the story of what his dad said to him when he was a kid.

"Chipper, you're lazy, and you'll never amount to anything."

He describes those words as "the phrase that wounded my soul." Those words marked him for years. The reminder that even his own dad didn't believe in him branded his chest. Ouch.

Question: "Whose words are you allowing to define you?"

Don't move past this question too quickly. Think about it.

Is there a conversation that happened years ago, perhaps when you were a kid, that marked your life?

Have you ever worn the label of lazy, a disappointment, or an accident? If so, where do you think that came from?

Better yet, who told you that?

> *"Then you will know the truth, and*
> *the truth will set you free."*
> —John 8:32

Back to my counselor for a moment. Chip challenges us to ask two questions when we find ourselves believing a lie.

1) "Where did that come from?"
2) "God, do You agree with that thought?"

When Chip took those questions to God, the response he heard was, "Chipper, I made you laid back and relaxed so that my hurting people would be comfortable talking to you."

That was the moment that Chip said he "switched fathers."

Maybe that is what you need today—a loving Father to speak truth over your life.

In the Gospel of Matthew, we get a ringside seat for the baptism of Jesus. We hear the voice of our heavenly Father speaking over His beloved Son:

> *As soon as Jesus was baptized, he went up out of the water. At that moment heaven was opened, and he saw the Spirit of God descending like a dove and alighting on him. And a voice from heaven said, "This is my Son, whom I love; with him I am well pleased."*
> *—Matthew 3:16-17*

This is my Son.

Whom I love.

With Him, I am well pleased.

Those are three powerful phrases.

Identity.

Affection.

Affirmation.

When the Father said, "This is my Son," He was speaking to Jesus's identity. Everybody who met Jesus had an opinion about who He was but only the Father knew His true identity.

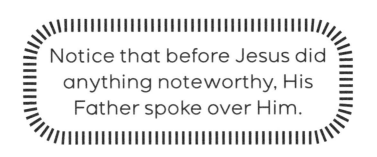

Notice that before Jesus did anything noteworthy, His Father spoke over Him.

The same is true for you.

Have you ever heard the Father speak to your true identity? Probably not. Most of us haven't because we are too busy listening to every other voice in our world.

Notice that before Jesus did anything noteworthy, His Father spoke over Him.

His identity didn't come from His accomplishments.

It didn't come from His approval ratings.

It didn't come from the win/loss column.

His identity came from His Father. PERIOD. Nothing can change that.

» You are not what you do.
» You are not what's been done to you.
» You are not what you hope to do.
» You are not who you think you are.
» You are not who others think you are.
» You are who the Father says you are.
» You are His son. You are His daughter.

Can you hear it? Now believe it.

The next thing the Father said was "whom I love."

FULLY ALIVE

Why is it so easy to accept that "God loves you" or maybe even "God loves the world" yet so difficult to accept that "God loves me"?

Is it because I know me?

My issues?

My deceptive ways?

My motives?

My thoughts?

Get this: He knows them too!

God knows everything about you.

E-v-e-r-y-t-h-i-n-g.

And still, He says, "This is my son/daughter, whom I love."

He knows and He loves.

He knows what nobody else knows . . . and He loves.

He knows what everybody knows . . . and He loves.

He knows the highlights and the lowlights . . . and He loves.

I don't know any other way to tell you . . . God the Father loves you. Whether you like it or not . . . you are loved.

The third set of words spoken over Jesus at His baptism was the simple statement, "With Him I am well pleased."

What would you do if you were convinced that the most important Being in the universe was not just pleased with you but "well pleased" with you?

Would you relax a bit?

Would you stop acting like the weight of the world was on your shoulders?

Would you take a day off?

FULLY ALIVE

Would you cut yourself some slack?

Would you quit jockeying for the next promotion?

He is not impressed with your title, salary, or influence. As a matter of fact, He is not "well pleased" with that. What pleases Him is that you know you are His, you know you are loved, and you live from that place.

Imagine that!

Try it on. Say this three times.

I am His. I am loved. He is pleased with me.
I am His. I am loved. He is pleased with me.
I am His. I am loved. He is pleased with me.

God doesn't just love you; He likes you. That is more than I can say for some people.

Regardless of how overwhelming or underwhelming your earthly father is or was, you have a heavenly Father who is crazy about you.

Do you need to go back to the previous chapter and read the story of the prodigal son again? I'll wait. . . .

Waiting . . .

 . . . waiting . . .

 . . . waiting . . .

 . . . still waiting . . .

You're back? Good . . . I missed you.

Talk it Over. Live it Out.

_____

1) What is "the truth" that this verse talks about?
   How does the truth set us free?
2) What specific memories or feelings do you asso-
   ciate with the idea of God as a father in your life?
3) In what ways do you believe God's presence
   or the concept of being fathered by God has
   influenced your personal development?
4) How do you address negative self-talk or criti-
   cism that conflicts with your understanding of
   your identity as a child of God?
5) What helps you feel secure in your identity and
   worth as someone fathered by God, especially
   when external validation is lacking?

REGARDLESS OF HOW
OVERWHELMING OR
UNDERWHELMING YOUR
EARTHLY FATHER IS OR WAS,
YOU HAVE A HEAVENLY FATHER
WHO IS CRAZY ABOUT YOU.

CHAPTER 6

FINANCIALLY FREE

Houston, we've had a problem here."
(I know, you're thinking the quote is, "Houston, we have a problem." I did too. You can look it up. The actual phrase from Command Module Pilot and astronaut, Jack Swigert, was, "Houston, we've had a problem here.")

Six words.

Six words the crew of the 1970 Apollo 13 never wanted to say.

On April 13, 1970, fifty-six hours into the mission to the moon, oxygen tank #2 exploded, causing damage to the control module.

"Houston, we've had a problem here."

Six words that saved their lives.

Problems. We've all got them. Nobody likes to admit them. The truth is you won't fix them until you face them.

Your finances?

"Houston, we've had a problem here."

According to debt.org, "American household debt hit a record $16.9 trillion at the end of 2022, up $2.75 trillion since 2019, according to the Federal Reserve. If you had to write that check it would read $16,960,000,000,000. Americans owe $986 billion on credit cards, surpassing the pre-pandemic high of $927 billion."[9]

YIKES!!

Now maybe YOU don't have a problem, but you probably know someone who does. I sure do.

In the words of Taylor Swift: "It's me, hi, I'm the problem, it's me."[10]

As soon as I was legally old enough to work, I got my first job at the age of fifteen. I didn't need a job but I wanted stuff, and so I got a J-O-B at Bed, Bath, and Beyond. I spent my summer earning

9   "Demographics of Debt," *Debt.org*, 4 Dec. 2023, https://www.debt.org/faqs/americans-in-debt/demographics/.
10   Taylor Swift, vocalist, "Anti-Hero," by Taylor Swift, released October 21, 2022, track 3 on *Midnights*, Republic.

$4.75 an hour as a cashier at the now bank-rupt BB&B. I didn't love working but I sure loved spending . . . so I worked.

I moved on to a job at a very upscale retirement home where I was a tuxedo-wearing busboy. (I told you it was upscale.) The best part of the job was commandeering a scooter to deliver food to residents' homes.

I'd crank that sucker to rabbit, and off I'd go. A few times, I forgot to put it back on turtle, and as you can imagine . . . whoops.

Next, I worked at a shoe store called The Athlete's Foot where I eventually became a manager.

Anyway, my point is, as soon as I could work, I did, and I haven't stopped since.

I'm willing to bet that you're not much different. Growing up, maybe you never thought much about the amount of time you'd spend at work to make money or to buy things . . . most of which you really don't need.

FULLY ALIVE

When my wife and I got married in the summer of 1998, we became one. I got all of her, and she got all of me.

I married her school loans, and she married my spending habits.

That is when we experienced what I call, "manageable debt." It was horrible, but it was manageable.

I learned early in our marriage that what you can't afford with cash you can with credit.

It's probably worth mentioning that every marriage seems to have a "saver" and a "spender." I'm sure you can figure out which is which in my scenario.

Shortly after getting married, I landed a job as a youth pastor making a full-time salary.

FULL-TIME SALARY!

I had never seen so much money. Almost $20k/year.

So, we bought a truck. A Chevy Z71 to be exact.

Three months later, we realized we couldn't afford the truck, the gas, or the insurance, so we down-sized the truck to a Honda Civic—and were intro-duced to something called "negative equity."

Negative equity = not cool. Basically, you owe more on something than the thing is worth.

Our "manageable debt" quickly became "out-of-control" debt.

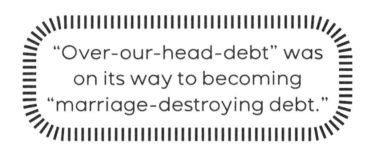

"Over-our-head-debt" was on its way to becoming "marriage-destroying debt."

Between spur-of-the-moment spending, opening new cards to get thirty days same as cash, not having a budget, and an inability to talk about our "problem," we were a mess.

Our bank account was frequently overdrawn as we hoped our paycheck would hit the account before our spending did.

"Out-of-control" turned into "over-our-head debt" pretty quickly.

We were spending more than we were making. Without realizing it, a large percentage of our income was going toward debt every month.

"Over-our-head-debt" was on its way to becoming "marriage-destroying debt."

I would secretly spend money and hide the purchase from my wife.

Let me tell you, secret spending will lead to not-so-secret resentment!

Add in poor communication, and you've got a recipe for disaster.

This was our reality.

For nine years.

Debt was eating our marriage for lunch!!

It was sucking the life out of us.

Debt destroyed any intimacy between us (kinda hard to be intimate with someone you are angry at).

One day I had had ENOUGH!

I was at a conference in Atlanta when I heard Dave Ramsey speak—correction—when I heard Dave Ramsey YELL!

I can't say exactly what snapped in me, but something did. I called my wife and told her that I was sorry and that I wanted us to talk when I got home.

This was the beginning of a new chapter.

My wife will tell you that she instantly felt hopeful.

We talked. We got on the same page. We got a plan. We got financial counseling.

For the next eighteen months, we clawed out of the mess that we had made.

We got to a place where we told our money where to go instead of wondering where it went.

HERE'S THE IRONY . . .

I spent my entire life in church. Do you know how many sermons about debt I recall? None! (Admittedly, I may not have been listening.)

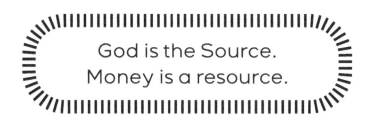

God is the Source.
Money is a resource.

Do you know how many people struggle with it? All of them!

Why isn't anybody talking about this?

The Bible talks about it.

In their book, *God and Money: How We Discovered True Riches at Harvard Business School*, authors John Cortines and Gregory Baumer tell the story of how businessman Howard Dayton categorized all verses about money and possessions in 1973. Dayton concluded:

> *There are 500 Bible verses pertaining to the topics of faith and prayer and yet 2,350 Bible verses on money. Why is that? Because God knows that our attitude toward money is an indication of where our heart is with God. We will either follow after gold or God and we cannot serve two masters. We will either turn to our wallet or our worship when we look to the source of our security. But we have to remember: Money is to be a resource, but it is not to be My Source.*[11]

God is the source. Money is a resource.

11   John Cortines and Gregory Baumer, *God and Money: How We Discovered True Riches at Harvard Business School* (Peabody, MA: Rose Publishing, 2016).

FULLY ALIVE

Pretend you are God for a minute.

As God, you know a thing or two about a thing or two.

You know your kids are going to spend the majority of their lives earning money. You also know that they are going to make dumb decisions along the way with money.

You know that the mismanagement of money will bring tremendous heartache into their lives, families, and future.

Knowing this, wouldn't it make sense that you would teach them principles on how to handle it?

Yes, yes you would, and that is EXACTLY what God has done in His Word: 2,350 of them. As Randy Alcorn says:

> *How could the Bible's Author and Editor justify devoting twice as many verses to money (about 2,350 of them) than to faith and prayer combined? How could*

Jesus say more about money than about both heaven and hell? Why did the Savior of the world spend 15 percent of his recorded words on this one subject? Why did he say more about how we are to view and handle money and possessions than about any other single thing?[12]

There is a throne in your life big enough for one.

Luke 16:13-14 (NLT) says:

"No one can serve two masters. For you will hate one and love the other; you will be devoted to one and despise the other. You cannot serve God and be enslaved to money." The Pharisees, who dearly loved their money, heard all this and scoffed at him.

"You cannot serve both God and money." Does anybody else think that this should say, "You

12   Randy Alcorn, *Money, Possessions, and Eternity: A Comprehensive Guide to What the Bible Says about Financial Stewardship, Generosity, Materialism, Retirement, Financial Planning, Gambling, Debt, and More* (Carol Stream, IL: Tyndale House Publishers, December 21, 2021).

cannot serve both God and Satan?" C'mon, what's the problem with money?

Nothing.

Money isn't the problem.

In the original language, this verse says, "You cannot serve both God and mammon."

What is mammon?

Mammon is the idol or the spirit of materialism.

The hunger for more.

The idea that your net worth determines your self-worth.

If you had more, you would be more.

"Mammon" was sometimes used to describe all lusts and excesses: gluttony, greed, and dishonest worldly gain.

Mammon promises what only God can provide.

Mammon promises security, freedom, power, and significance.

Mammon says:

- » If I had more, I would have peace.
- » If I had more, I wouldn't need this job.
- » If I had more, I would be somebody.
- » If I had more, I'd get more respect.
- » The spirit of money stands in opposition to the Spirit of God.

Money is sneaky. Many of us don't even realize that we've given over the authority of our lives to materialism.

Financial freedom begins
when debt is evicted
and God is enthroned.

Can I ask you, "Who is sitting on the throne of your life?" Be honest.

Stats say:

- » About 80% of Americans worry daily about money.[13]
- » Over 70% of American households live from paycheck to paycheck.[14]
- » Close to half of marriages that in end in divorce cite "financial problems" as a primary reason for the demise.[15]

The reason so many of us are worrying, stressing, and fighting is because debt has never been evicted, and God is not on the throne.

FINANCIAL FREEDOM BEGINS WHEN DEBT IS EVICTED, AND GOD IS ENTHRONED.

---

13   "Survey: 80% of Americans say financial situation causes high anxiety," *NewsNation*, https://www.newsnationnow.com/business/your-money/americans-financial-situation-anxiety-survey/#:~:text=Survey%3A%2080%25%20of%20Americans%20cite,as%20cause%20of%20high%20anxiety,

14   Jacob Wade, "This Generation Is Surprisingly Most Likely to Live Paycheck to Paycheck," *News & Insights*, 25 January 2024, https://www.nasdaq.com/articles/this-generation-is-surprisingly-most-likely-to-live-paycheck-to-paycheck#.

15   Christy Bieber, "Revealing Divorce Statistics in 2024," *Forbes*, 5 Feb. 2024, www.forbes.com/advisor/legal/divorce/divorce-statistics/.

Let's talk about debt, and then let's talk about God.

DEBT ISN'T SINFUL, BUT IT CAN BE STRESSFUL.

Can I get an amen?

Debt is tricky.

Nobody graduates college and thinks, *Let me rack up as much debt as possible.* But it happens. Often.

Debt is easy to get into and hard to get out of.

Debt creates the ability to buy what you otherwise could not afford.

Debt is spending tomorrow's money—today.

The ultimate reason that debt is stressful is because it makes you a servant to someone other than God.

"The rich rule over the poor, and the borrower is slave to the lender."
—Proverbs 22:7

When we "borrow" money, we literally place ourselves in contractual bondage to the lender. We give up a certain amount of "financial freedom."

I'm not telling you to never borrow money. Please don't hear what I'm not saying.

It is not a sin for you to take out a loan or put your gas on a credit card, but with each "loan" comes a degree of stress.

The greater the debt, the greater the stress.

Debt is an appetite that must be starved. You cannot spend your way out of debt.

In my case, I was robbing my future to pay for my present. The problem I found was that "future me" was broke because "present me" had already spent the money. It is an easy cycle to fall into. Spend today, and figure it out tomorrow.

If you are in debt, which most people are, let me give you two thoughts.

Thought #1: Stop feeding it.

Debt is an appetite that must be starved. You cannot spend your way out of debt.

Dave Ramsey calls it the "Law of Holes." The "Law of Holes" is simple—when you're in one, stop digging.

Nobody gets out of debt by getting into more debt.

Thought #2: Get a plan.

One of the most humbling moments of my life was talking to a financial counselor. He started asking questions about our current reality, and I had nobody to blame but myself.

We were so emotionally attached to our circumstances that we needed *outside insight*.

Outside insight is perspective from someone who is not emotionally attached to your circumstances.

We needed it.

And you probably do as well.

Hear me when I say this: getting in debt is easy; getting out of debt takes work.

One incredibly helpful tool for me and my wife as we started the process of paying down debt is something called a "Debt Payoff Spectacular" from iwasbrokenowimnot.com.[16]

It didn't take long for the excitement to fade and for Mammon to fight back, so every month we

---

16   "Pay-Off Spectaculars," I Was Broke. Now I'm Not., accessed May 28, 2024, https://www. iwasbrokenowimnot.com/tools-spectaculars.

would color in our Debt Payoff Spectaculars to keep the progress in front of us. As a matter of fact, our fridge was covered in these things.

1) Car Loan
2) Credit Card
3) Overdraft
4) School Loans

Hanging beside our kids' artwork were our spectaculars for all to see.

Quit wondering where your money has gone, and start telling it where to go.

If debt is eating your lunch, the first thing you've got to do is create a plan, and be honest about where you are. Quit wondering where your money has gone, and start telling it where to go.

One last nugget before we move on to God.

When we got serious about getting out of consumer debt, we were advised that it would be a twenty-four-month journey. We'd have to make some serious changes.

We stopped going out to eat. We cut unnecessary expenses. We put as much money as possible toward retiring debt.

It was a long process but not as long as we had anticipated. We fast-tracked the twenty-four months into eighteen! Yes, we paid off all our consumer debt in eighteen months.

Insert happy dance.

Now, let's talk about God.

Whether you've realized it or not, money is a God issue.

As long as money is on the throne, God is not.

The Bible makes it clear that God is the Author of all things, Creator of all things, and over all things. Yet, when it comes to finances, most people don't put God in His rightful place.

GOD'S PLACE IS FIRST PLACE

This is where I talk to you about a churchy word called the "tithe." Not "tides." Sounds crazy but we used to have an individual who would write this on the bottom of their check in the subject line: "tides."

What is a tithe? Simply put, a tithe is a tenth— one-tenth or 10 percent.

For example, if you had ten slices of pizza, and I asked for a tithe, I would be asking for one slice.

FULLY ALIVE

When it comes to the Bible, the principle of the tithe is to return 10 percent of my income to God through my local church.

Say what? Don't stop reading. Hear me out.

Churches have gotten a bad rep for preaching about the tithe. I'll admit, if the only time your church talks about money is a message on tithing, I'd be a little suspect myself.

There is so much more I could say about finances, but I'm a big fan of short books.

The Bible teaches about saving, investing, lending, inheritance, debt, and many other topics that we can talk about at a later date. For now, let's stay on topic.

Let me address the elephant in the room.

If I am barely getting by on 100 percent of my income, how in the world am I supposed to give away 10 percent of it?

I get it. The math doesn't add up.

Let me establish a few ideas.

1) God is the Author of all blessings.

As a matter of fact, God had Moses remind His people that although they worked hard, it was actually God who was giving them the ability to generate wealth.

You may say to yourself, "My power and the strength of my hands have produced this wealth for me."

That's not what the Word of God teaches:

> *"But remember the Lord your God, for it is he who gives you the ability to produce wealth, and so confirms his covenant, which he swore to your ancestors, as it is today."*
> —Deuteronomy 8:18

2) God is the Owner of all things.

What this means is that although my name may be on the title of my car and on the desk in my office, I'm just borrowing it from the Lord.

"The earth is the LORD's, and everything in it, the world, and all who live in it."
—Psalm 24:1

3) If God is the Owner, I must be the manager.

Let me ask you what you would do if you employed a manager who was mismanaging your business. Would you promote them? No way! You'd warn them, and then you'd fire them. Think about that from the perspective of God as the owner and you and me as the managers.

"Whoever can be trusted with very little can also be trusted with much, and whoever is dishonest with very little will also be dishonest with much."
—Luke 16:10

4) Tithing is returning.

It is called returning because you can't "give" what doesn't belong to you. God has entrusted us with wealth and expects us to manage it according to His instructions.

> *"A tithe of everything from the land, whether grain from the soil or fruit from the trees,* belongs *to the Lord; it is holy to the Lord."*
> —Leviticus 27:30 (author emphasis added)

Imagine for a second that I borrow your surfboard and never return it. What would you call that?

Yup. Your words, not mine.

5) The tithe is the first 10 percent.

Remember, God's place is first place. When we put Him first, we become obedient to His commands. In essence, our obedience says, "I trust You, God, to provide for my needs."

FULLY ALIVE

"Honor the LORD with your wealth, with the firstfruits of all your crops; then your barns will be filled to overflowing, and your vats will brim over with new wine."
—Proverbs 3:9-10

Notice the cause-and-effect nature of this verse. Honor and obey, then you will be blessed.

Blessing follows obedience. Not the other way around.

Too often we put the cart before the horse and ask God to bless us so we can obey Him. It doesn't work that way.

It takes faith to give first.

Most people would agree that God should be in first place in our lives. But then you bring up the topic of finances and they begin to make excuses.

Either you trust God, or you don't.

It's wild to me to think that people can trust God with their eternity but not their reality!

Let's get practical for a second.

1) When you create your budget, list the tithe first.
2) When you put God first, it causes you to reorient the rest of your spending around your priorities.
3) When you do this and payday comes around, tithing is not an emotional decision. You've already spent it on paper before spending it in reality.
4) The tithe is paid to the local church.

In the Old Testament of the Bible, the tithe was brought to the priests in the temple. In the New Testament, it was brought to the local church.

> *"I the LORD do not change. So you, the descendants of Jacob, are not destroyed. Ever since the time of your ancestors you have turned away from my decrees and have not kept them. Return to me,*

*and I will return to you," says the L*ᴏʀᴅ
Almighty. —Malachi 3:6-7

But you ask, "How are we to return?" Refer to Malachi 3:8-12:

> *"Will a mere mortal rob God? Yet you*
> *rob me. But you ask, 'How are we rob-*
> *bing you?' In tithes and offerings. You*
> *are under a curse—your whole nation—*
> *because you are robbing me. Bring the*
> *whole tithe into the storehouse, that*
> *there may be food in my house. Test me*
> *in this," says the L*ᴏʀᴅ *Almighty, "and see*
> *if I will not throw open the floodgates of*
> *heaven and pour out so much blessing*
> *that there will not be room enough*
> *to store it. I will prevent pests from*
> *devouring your crops, and the vines in*
> *your fields will not drop their fruit before*
> *it is ripe," says the L*ᴏʀᴅ *Almighty. "Then*
> *all the nations will call you blessed, for*
> *yours will be a delightful land," says*
> *the L*ᴏʀᴅ *Almighty.*

When we apply this principle, we literally put our money where our mouth is.

I like to think of it like this. Every time I get paid, I take a test.

Do I trust God, and can God trust me?

When I put Him first, He promises to open the floodgates of heaven and pour out so much blessing that I can't store it all. Then He promises to protect what I do possess, and finally, those around us will call us blessed because our land will be delightful.

Could it be that a major reason our nation is in such a mess is that we have been neglecting this very principle?

People have questions anytime I teach on this principle. Here are a few of them.

1) Isn't the tithe part of the Old Testament law?

Yes and no. Yes, it was part of the law. No, the principle of the tithe was established six hundred years before the law was written.

The tithe is a prelaw concept. Abraham tithed to Melchizedek in Genesis 14:20. Jacob vowed to tithe in Genesis 28:20-22.

Jesus validated it.

In Matthew 23:23, Jesus reprimands the Pharisees and says:

> *"Woe to you, teachers of the law and Pharisees, you hypocrites! You give a tenth of your spices—mint, dill and cumin. But you have neglected the more important matters of the law—justice, mercy and faithfulness. You should have practiced the latter, without neglecting the former."*

Every example of New Testament giving goes beyond the tithe.

The tithe was never intended to be a lid but rather a launchpad of generosity.

2) I can't afford to tithe.

Let's be honest, many who say, "I have nothing to give," spend large amounts of discretionary income on cars, clothes, coffee, entertainment, phones, computers, and so on. They have nothing to give when they're done spending, precisely because they're never done spending.

Too many people are praying for a financial miracle when what they really need is a budget!

FULLY ALIVE

The real issue is that we haven't been faithful with a little, so we'll never be entrusted with much.

Too many people are praying for a financial miracle when what they really need is a budget!

If you can't trust God where you are now, what makes you think you will trust Him when you have more?

Start where you are.

Money magazine called Sir John Templeton, the billionaire founder of the Templeton Group, "arguably the greatest global stock picker of the century."[17] He was knighted by Queen Elizabeth II for his generosity.

It is estimated that he gave away over $1 billion in his lifetime. Templeton passed away in 2008 at the age of ninety-five. Templeton called tithing the "single best investment" anyone can make.

17   Money Magazine cited in "Sir John Templeton: From Stock Picker to Philanthropist," *Value Investor Academy*, 10 July 2023, https://valueinvestoracademy.com/sir-john-templeton-from-stock-picker-to-philanthropist/#:~:text=Sir%20John%20Templeton%2C%20was%20called,phenomenal%20success%20throughout%20his%20career.

He said, "I have observed 100,000 families over my years of investment counseling. I always saw greater prosperity and happiness among those families who tithed than among those who didn't."

Dream with me for a second.

What would it feel like to not have financial pressure?

Imagine for a second what you could do and would do if you didn't have the current stress of debt in your life.

What would you do?

For real, think about it. Don't rush through this chapter just because the end is in sight.

Write down three things you think you'd do if you were financially free.

Here's a mind-blowing lesson that I've learned.

FULLY ALIVE

Two years will be here whether you like it or not. You can either be where you want to be, or you can be in the same situation you are in right now.

"The best time to plant a tree was 20 years ago. The second best time is today."
—Chinese Proverb

"Start planting."
—Me

Talk it Over. Live it Out.

"No one can serve two masters. Either you will hate the one and love the other, or you will be devoted to the one and despise the other. You cannot serve both God and money."
—Luke 16:13

---

1) What pivotal moments in your own financial journey led you to where you are today?
2) How have your spending habits evolved over time, from your first job to your current financial situation?
3) In what ways do you think societal attitudes towards money impact personal financial decisions?
4) What stands out to you about this verse? Have you ever tried to serve two masters?
5) What is the significance of Jesus's use of money as a master in this verse?

GOD IS THE SOURCE.
MONEY IS A RESOURCE.

CHAPTER 7

FILLED WITH THE SPIRIT

O ur church was four years old.
We had broken several growth barriers.

We had moved into larger facilities. Internet articles had been written about us.

I was given the "church planter of the year" award from my alma mater.

And I was exhausted.

I'll never forget the Sunday I quit.

That day, I came home after what I thought was a good Sunday.

Attendance, good.

Volunteer teams, good.

Energy, good.

Worship, good.

Message, obviously good.

FULLY ALIVE

I had one conversation that unearthed something not-so-good in me. My leadership was challenged. The direction of our church was questioned. And I felt exposed.

For years, I knew I wasn't the strongest leader. As a matter of fact, one of my mentors *told* me I wasn't a strong leader.

It hurt. It was honest. It marked me.

But I thought that the success around me must validate the leader within me. It didn't.

When I got home, I stormed into my bedroom closet and had the most honest conversation with God that I had ever had. I laid into Him. I gave it to Him good. And He took it. All of it.

I told God that I never signed up for this. I was perfectly happy to stay where I was. Starting a church was His idea, not mine.

I didn't feel qualified to be in my role. I felt like the weight of the church was on my shoulders, and I had to carry it. I had to be creative. I had to have new sermon ideas every seven days.

EVERY SEVEN DAYS!!!

So in that closet, I did it. I finally did it.

I quit.

I told God that if this is what ministry is like, He could take it and shove it! I didn't want it, and I quit.

That's when I felt God say, *It's about time.*

What?

Then I heard, *Maybe you'll let Me lead now.*

I was confused . . . and hungry, so I came out of the bedroom closet and chewed on that thought:

It's about time. Maybe you'll let Me lead now.

That showdown with God did something to me. It caused me to notice leaders who have been at it longer than me and are happy and healthy with thriving families and churches.

I swallowed my pride and began to ask them what their secret was.

One after another, they told me that the secret was their relationship with the Holy Spirit.

That wasn't good enough for me.

I knew there must be more. What's your schedule like? When is your study day? When is your staff meeting? What does your org chart look like? How often do you take a vacation? How far out is your planning?

Nope. None of that.

I was confused.

Through those conversations, I learned that my understanding of the Holy Spirit was inaccurate. I was under the impression that the Holy Spirit was active in the writing of the Scriptures and the founding of the early church but not anymore.

Maybe it was the church I grew up in. Maybe it was my college professors. Probably it was my lack of listening and study. When it came to the Holy Spirit, I was ignorant.

I had some holy hang-ups about the Holy Spirit.

For what it's worth, I wasn't completely ignorant to the Holy Spirit, but what I thought I knew was really weird.

For instance, I remember attending a church in college where an elderly lady just fell down while singing—and nobody moved a muscle. Nobody!

I was freaked out. I wasn't sure whether to call 911, check for a pulse, or get the defibrillator. A few minutes later, she came to and stood back up. Nobody talked about it.

At a camp I worked at in college, I had a group of ladies come in for a retreat. As they planned the weekend, they talked about being slain in the Spirit and needed to be sure they had catchers in place.

I only caught for a few years in Little League, so I didn't volunteer.

I could go on, but you get it. I had some holy hang-ups about the Holy Spirit.

So, to make a long story short, I realized I had been relying on my own creativity and my own leadership and my own strength to do my job.

And I was empty.

Dry.

Exhausted.

Frustrated.

Desperate times call for desperate measures, and I was finally desperate.

I remember attending a conference for pastors called The Healthy Pastors Conference. It sounded like something I needed.

I went into this conference telling God that I was open. I wanted everything that He had for me. Most of all, I wanted to see what the Holy Spirit was all about.

I went forward for prayer every chance I could get. I didn't want to get slain, but I was open to it.

I was open to people sharing special words from God for me. I was even open to speaking in tongues if that was something God had for me.

None of that happened.

But something did happen.

I started noticing things. I felt like the burden of leading had been lifted. I started seeing the Holy Spirit all through Scripture.

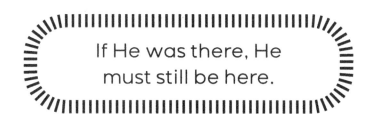

If He was there, He must still be here.

In creating the world, the Spirit was there. He was empowering prophets in the Old Testament. In the New Testament, He was all over the place.

For the baptism of Jesus, He was there. For the launching of the church, He was there. During persecution, He was there.

The Holy Spirit was all over the place, trans-forming men and women of God.

If He was there, He must still be here.

If you are worn down and tired, I get it. I was there.

Can I give you a crash course on what I learned about the Holy Spirit?

In the Gospel of Luke, we get to eavesdrop on a conversation between Jesus and His closest friends.

At this point in the story, Jesus has gone to the cross, died, and been resurrected!

He has spent forty days teaching His disciples what they are to do once He is gone. These are some of the final words of Jesus. Check it out:

> *"I am going to send you what my Father has promised; but stay in the city until you have been clothed with power from on high." When he had led them out to the vicinity of Bethany, he lifted up his hands and blessed them. While he was blessing them, he left them and*

was taken up into heaven. Then they worshiped him and returned to Jerusalem with great joy. And they stayed continually at the temple, praising God. —Luke 24:49-53

Now, let's go to the book of Acts. Acts is a sequel to the Luke written by the same author and includes the same story:

In my former book, Theophilus [friend of God], I wrote about all that Jesus began to do and to teach until the day he was taken up to heaven, after giving instructions through the Holy Spirit to the apostles he had chosen. After his suffering, he presented himself to them and gave many convincing proofs that he was alive. He appeared to them over a period of forty days and spoke about the kingdom of God. On one occasion, while he was eating with them, he gave them this command: "Do not leave Jerusalem, but wait for the gift my Father promised, which you have heard me speak about. For John baptized with water, but in a few days you will be baptized with the Holy Spirit." —Acts 1:1-5 (author emphasis)

Remember that word *wait.*

"But you will receive power when the Holy Spirit comes on you; and you will be my witnesses in Jerusalem, and in all Judea and Samaria, and to the ends of the earth." After he said this, he was taken up before their very eyes, and a cloud hid him from their sight. —Acts1:8-9

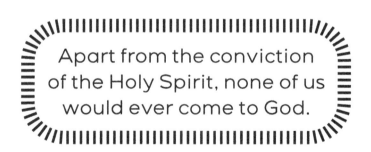

Apart from the conviction of the Holy Spirit, none of us would ever come to God.

Spark Notes version:

- » I [Jesus] want to cover you with power from on high.
- » I have a gift for you.
- » Stay in Jerusalem and wait for the gift I have for you.
- » You will be baptized in the Holy Spirit.
- » You will receive power to be My witness to the world.
- » He left them.

Later, you see this very thing unfold in chapter 2. The disciples wait in Jerusalem, and God pours out His Spirit.

A literal transformation happens in their lives.

One of the disciples, named Peter, preaches his first sermon, and three thousand people get saved and baptized.

I don't know how much you know about Peter, but this poor guy couldn't do anything right.

He's the one who tried to rebuke Jesus and got called Satan.

He's also the one who chopped an ear off when Jesus was arrested. But now—filled with the Holy Spirit—Peter preaches and three thousand people respond.

THE HOLY SPIRIT EMPOWERS ME TO BE WHO I WAS CREATED TO BE AND TO DO WHAT I WAS CREATED TO DO.

Apart from the conviction of the Holy Spirit, none of us would ever come to God. It's impossible.

What this means is that we can never experience our true identity in Christ as sons and daughters of God without the work of the Holy Spirit.

You were also created for a purpose.

Even if you don't know it yet. You have a purpose.

Your purpose is bigger than you are which is why you'll never accomplish it in your own ability.

You need to be empowered by the Holy Spirit.

> *"But you will receive power when*
> *the Holy Spirit comes on you."*
> —Acts 1:8

The word translated "power" is the Greek word, *dunamis.* It is where we get the word for dynamite. It is an explosive power. God wants to gift you with a power to fulfill all the plans He has for you.

I've found that the call of God on my life is intimidating. Maybe you feel the same?

But if God calls you to it, He will empower you to do it!

Repeat after me:

I CANNOT ACCOMPLISH HIS PURPOSE IN MY STRENGTH.

Let me close this chapter with three reasons why you NEED the Holy Spirit in your life.

1) You cannot live a full life without Him.

Way too many "Christians" are living way below the purpose and call on their lives. Hear me when I say that God did not send His Son to die on a cross so that we could get saved and then go through life defeated.

2) You will never use what you don't know you have.

If this chapter is new information to you, you might want to go back and read it again.

I was a Christian for almost thirty years before I learned about and received the gift of the Holy Spirit in my life.

I remember telling my friend Tim that I felt like I had been push mowing my grass my entire life.

I hate yard work. It brings me no joy. It is hot, sweaty, and boring.

Anyway, I told Tim that I was exhausted and felt like I couldn't do it anymore.

At the moment of throwing in the towel, someone approached me and showed me a lever on the handle of my mower. He said that if I pull the lever the mower will actually go on its own. All I've got to do is walk behind it.

Are you kidding me?

All my life I've been pushing and wearing myself out when the power was at my fingertips all along!

3) Greater is He that is in you than he that is in the world.

"You, dear children, are from God and have overcome them, because the one who is in you is greater than the one who is in the world."
—1 John 4:4

There is a myth that floats around the church quite a bit because it sounds good: "God will never give you more than you can handle." Sounds great.

Too bad it's not true.

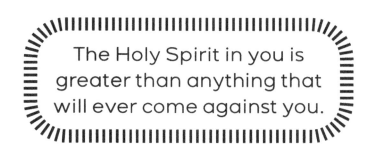

The Holy Spirit in you is greater than anything that will ever come against you.

I've searched for that verse, and it's just not there. The truth is this: *"God will never allow more on you than what He has put IN you!"*

The Holy Spirit in you is greater than anything that will ever come against you.

The great news is that the Holy Spirit is available to you right here, right now.

The only prerequisite to receiving the baptism of the Holy Spirit is to first repent of your sins and receive Jesus as your Lord and Savior. (If you skipped chapter 1, go back and read it.)

Once you've done that, just ask God the Father to fill you with His Spirit.

> *"If you then, though you are evil, know how to give good gifts to your children, how much more will your Father in heaven give the Holy Spirit to those who ask him!"*
> *—Luke 11:13*

If you're not sure what to pray, here is a simple prayer you can use.

> *Heavenly Father, thank You for the gift of the Holy Spirit. I ask You right now to fill me with Your Holy Spirit. Baptize me and empower me for what You have created me to do today. Amen.*

Talk it Over. Live it Out.

"I am going to send you what my Father has promised; but stay in the city until you have been clothed with power from on high."
—Luke 24:49

---

1) Have you ever struggled with impatience in waiting for God's timing or direction in your life? How did you learn to trust in His timing and surrender control?

2) Consider the three reasons outlined in this chapter for why you need the Holy Spirit in your life. Which reason resonates with you the most? Why?

3) How can you actively cultivate a deeper reliance on the Holy Spirit in your daily life?

4) How have you relied on God's strength during seasons of exhaustion?

5) What misconceptions or "holy hang-ups" have you encountered regarding the Holy Spirit in your own life or within your religious community?

THE HOLY SPIRIT IN
YOU IS GREATER THAN
ANYTHING THAT WILL EVER
COME AGAINST YOU.

CHAPTER 8

FORMED FOR A PURPOSE

As we wrap up our journey, you need to know that you have been formed for a purpose.

In Psalm 139:13, David the shepherd and soon-to-be king wrote these words:

> *"For you created my inmost being;*
> *you knit me together in my mother's womb."*

If anybody lived with the tension of knowing that they were made for more, it had to be David. He had the privilege of learning early in life what his calling was—to be king.

One small problem: he was the furthest thing from king.

He was just a small-town boy, the youngest of eight brothers, a singer, songwriter, and shepherd. If the purpose of his life was to become king and lead God's people, it would take a miracle to make it happen.

Good news—God is in the miracle business.

FULLY ALIVE

Not only does God create us for a purpose, but He also knits us together to accomplish that purpose.

Have you ever knit anything before? I have. I knit a hat with a contraption called the Nifty-Knitter. It was tedious.

Knit after knit and knot after knot. It takes some serious time. I can promise you that nobody knits on accident. God didn't accidentally knit you.

God has uniquely knit and gifted you for a specific calling that is on your life. You are not an accident.

God has a purpose and a plan for your life.

Many have credited Mark Twain for this quote, and it couldn't be more fitting:

> *"The two greatest days of a person's life are the day they are born and the day they discover why."*

You've probably got a certificate in a filing cabinet somewhere with your date of birth on it. Most people know when they were born, but many people don't know why they were born.

Do you?

Don't you wish someone would just tell you early in life what you are supposed to do WITH your life?

"Congrats on graduating sixth grade! These are your strengths, and this is what you should do with them."

How easy would that be! Instead, most of us spend the majority of our lives wondering what our purpose in life is.

What is my purpose?

Why am I here?

Does my life matter?

I want you to know that YES, your life matters.

Unfortunately, I can't tell you specifically what your purpose is, but I do believe that examining your strengths, weaknesses, hang-ups, and hurts will help you figure it out.

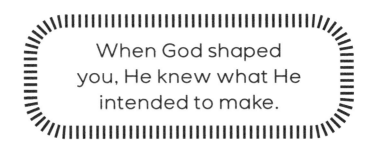

When God shaped you, He knew what He intended to make.

In the Old Testament, the prophet Jeremiah had a difficult time wrapping his mind around the fact that God had a purpose for him:

> *The word of the L*ORD *came to me, saying,*
> *"Before I formed you in the womb I knew you, before you were born I set you apart; I appointed you as a prophet to the nations."*
> *"Alas, Sovereign L*ORD*," I said, "I do not know how to speak; I am too young." But*

> *the Lord said to me, "Do not say, 'I am too young.' You must go to everyone I send you to and say whatever I command you. Do not be afraid of them, for I am with you and will rescue you," declares the Lord. —Jeremiah 1:4-8 (author emphasis added)*

The word used here, "formed," is the Hebrew word *yatsar*. It means to form, to make, or to shape.

A good example would be a potter *yatsar-ing* (I just made up that word.) a pot. When a potter sits down at her wheel, she knows the type of pot she intends to make.

In the same way, when God shaped you, He knew what He intended to make.

You were shaped for a purpose.

Pastor Rick Warren, founding pastor of Saddleback Church, developed an acrostic to help assess our purpose using the word "S.H.A.P.E."

Let's try it on.

S–Spiritual Gifts

We've already discussed how God places the Holy Spirit inside us when we put our faith and trust in Jesus for our salvation. You also need to know is that the Holy Spirit supernaturally gifts us to fulfill the purpose on our lives.

Think about it. Doesn't it make sense that God would gift us for what He has created us to do?

In 1 Corinthians 12:1, the apostle Paul says, "Now about the gifts of the Spirit, brothers and sisters, I do not want you to be uninformed." If you keep reading 1 Corinthians 12, you will find a breakdown of the gifts God gives us.

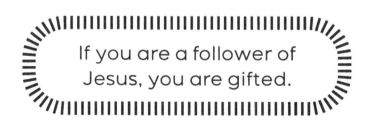

If you are a follower of Jesus, you are gifted.

Here is a quick list of the gifts found in 1 Corinthians 12:

» Words of wisdom: Supernatural insight to advise others
» Words of knowledge: Supernatural understanding of God's will and Word
» Faith: Supernatural ability to believe and trust God
» Healing: Supernatural ability to heal and restore mind, body, and emotions
» Miracles: Supernatural ability to perform miracles
» Prophecy: Supernatural ability to build up and encourage fellow believers
» Discerning of spirits: Supernatural ability to distinguish between good and evil spirits
» Tongues and interpretation of tongues: Supernatural ability to speak in or understand a heavenly language

We don't have time today to dig deeper than this, but I need you to know that if you are a follower of Jesus, you are gifted.

First Corinthians 12 also teaches us that while each of our gifts is different, they are complimentary. I need your gift, and you need mine.

The imagery that Paul uses is that of a body. Each part is unique and necessary.

It would be foolish for the foot to think that it is unimportant because it is not a hand.

I mean, have you ever woken up in the night only to find that your foot was still asleep? We'd all agree that the foot is important.

You are gifted.

Your gift is important.

Your gift works.

Work your gift.

Q: What has God supernaturally gifted you to do?

H–Heart

Let me ask you a few questions:

- » What fires you up?
- » What breaks your heart?
- » What gets your heart racing?
- » What makes you angry?
- » What do you notice that others do not?
- » What do you care about that others don't?

The Bible uses the word "heart" to describe your desires, hopes, dreams, and ambitions. Your heart is the central operating system of your life.

Jesus says that everything we do starts in our hearts (see Matthew 15:10), and "For out of the overflow of the heart, the mouth speaks" (Luke 6:45, BSB).

The passions of your heart tend to point toward your purpose.

Q: What are you passionate about?

FULLY ALIVE

A-Abilities

> *"I don't even have any good skills. You know like nunchuck skills, bowhunting skills, computer hacking skills. Girls only want boyfriends who have great skills."*[18]
> —Napoleon Dynamite

What are your skills? What abilities do you possess that come naturally to you?

Studies have proven that the average person has between 500 and 700 different skills and abilities. That is a lot of skills.

Many people overlook their abilities because they almost seem effortless to us.

Maybe you have:

- » Athletic abilities . . . sports come easy.
- » Musical abilities . . . music makes sense.
- » Mechanical abilities . . . how things work.
- » Design abilities . . . why and how things fit together.

---

18   Jared Hess, *Napoleon Dynamite* (January 17, 2004; Los Angeles, CA: Fox Searchlight Pictures).

» Administration abilities . . . organization is easy.

Here's a good exercise.

Ask two people who have known you for a few years to make a short list of things that you are good at. It's amazing what a little "outside insight" will reveal about us.

Now that you've identified a few skills and abilities, it's time to use them for God's glory and our good, like Paul instructs in 1 Corinthians 10:31: "So whether you eat or drink or whatever you do, do it all for the glory of God."

Q: What talents and skills do I have?

P-Personality

Do you love meeting new people? Would you prefer to keep to yourself? Do you appreciate variety, or would you rather stick to a routine? Are you a thinker or a feeler? Introvert or extrovert?

Our personality is the byproduct of many of these things. While our upbringing assists in crafting our personality, much of it is hardwired into us by our Creator.

There is no right or wrong personality. If you are an introvert, don't wish you were an extrovert. If you are a feeler, don't downplay your feelings.

You are wired the way you are on purpose; it is all part of your design.

Knowing your personality helps you to figure out what jobs, roles, and areas of service will make you live fully alive.

Q: How am I wired?

E-Experiences
Like it or not, our experiences shape all of us.

Good ones and bad ones.

You are the result of a million moments woven together. For better or worse, your family experiences have made you who you are.

Your education has played a role in shaping you.

Each job you've had and will have contributed to your development.

Your successes and failures have added to the sum of who and where you are in life.

The reason your experiences play a role in shaping your purpose is that God will use all the raw materials of your life to serve others around you.

> *"We might impress people with our strengths, but we connect with people through our weaknesses."*[19]
> —Craig Groeschel

19   Craig Groeschel, X post, September 3, 2013, 11:34 am, https://x.com/craiggroeschel/status/374918426327650304?lang=en.

FULLY ALIVE

In 1996, I was sitting on the steps of a cabin at a summer camp called Master's Inn when I said something I couldn't believe I said.

I was a student at Liberty University and had recently switched majors from business to ministry. I was working that summer as a camp director for elementary-age students.

Most kids arrived full of sugar and excitement . . . but not Cory.

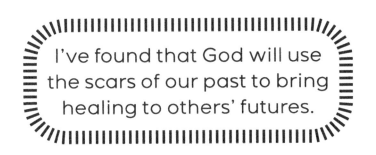

I've found that God will use the scars of our past to bring healing to others' futures.

I spotted this one young boy sitting on the steps of his cabin with a look of sadness on his face. I sat down next to Cory and asked him what was going on.

As it turns out, his parents were separating, and they thought it was a good idea to drop that bomb on him on the way to camp.

Out of my mouth came the words, "I know what you're going through." I never use those words. Most of the time when people use those words, they have no idea what others are going through, but I did know what he was going through.

The reason I know is because my parents separated when I was his age. I knew the hurt. I knew what it was like to wonder what you did to make them separate.

I knew the knot in the stomach. I knew what it was like to walk into Mom and Dad's room only to remember Dad wasn't there.

I knew it, and I knew it all too well.

That week I was able to use my painful past to bring hope to Cory.

"The Father of compassion and the God of all comfort, who comforts us in all our troubles, so that we can comfort those in any trouble with the comfort we ourselves receive from God."
—2 Corinthians 1:3-4

God never wastes a hurt. He will bring purpose from the pain. I've found that God will use the scars of our past to bring healing to others' futures.

Don't run from your past.

Embrace your experiences.

Use them to serve others.

Q: What experiences have I had that can help others?

Knowing your S.H.A.P.E. is the one step to finding your purpose. The next is to do something with it. Find your place.

Just as the body has unique parts and a team has unique positions, the church has distinct roles for each of us.

God designed you to bring your Spiritual Gifts, Heart, Abilities, Passions, and Experiences alongside like-minded people to impact the world.

Imagine the frustration of putting together a 1,000-piece puzzle only to be missing a few pieces.

Or what about whipping up your favorite recipe only to discover you're out of one key ingredient That puzzle will never be complete, and that recipe won't be the same without all the parts.

Church is the same way.

I want to encourage you to find and join a local church where you can use your gifts alongside others. You are a piece of the puzzle. You are the spice to their recipe.

You were created for this.

Step out and
watch God step in.

If you are new to this "fully alive" way of living, don't let it intimidate you. We all were once new. Take a step and watch God meet you there.

> *"From him the whole body, joined and held together by every supporting ligament, grows and builds itself up in love, as each part does its work."*
> —Ephesians 4:16

You are created to be part of something bigger—God's family. He has a seat at the table with your name on it, and He's got a role for you to play.

Step out, and watch God step in.

Talk it Over. Live it Out.

"For you created my inmost being;
you knit me together in my mother's womb."
—Psalm 139:13

---

1) How do you approach the process of discerning and fulfilling your purpose?
2) Have you ever felt a sense of uncertainty or confusion about your purpose?
3) How does the verse above influence how you feel about yourself and others?
4) Which aspect of your S.H.A.P.E. do you feel most confident in? Which do you think requires further exploration or development?
5) What experience from your past has shaped your understanding of your purpose or calling? How have you used this experience to positively impact others?

WHEN GOD SHAPED
YOU, HE KNEW WHAT
HE INTENDED TO MAKE.

CLOSING THOUGHTS

Driving home from a friend's wedding I get a call from my neighbor,

"Hey, man, are you home?" he asks.

"No, I'm on my way home from Charlotte, what's up?"

He responds, "My garage got broken into last night and my and your son's dirt bikes were stolen."

My heart sank. My son had recently cleaned up his bike to list it for sale. He is going to be crushed!

All we knew was that at some point in the night, someone had crowbarred my neighbor's door and stolen two dirt bikes.

Police had been contacted. An investigation was underway.

My wife and I were driving, so there wasn't much we could do until we got home.

I then receive another call from my neighbor.

FULLY ALIVE

He informed me that he had hidden an Apple AirTag on his bike to track it in the event it was lost or stolen. They could see that the bikes had been taken two hours away to a larger city.

My wife starts pulling up traffic cameras on her phone in hopes of spotting a trailer with the two dirt bikes on it.

I thought she was crazy.

I was right. It yielded no results.

However, that AirTag did.

The police were able to find the house and seize the bikes, and my son and neighbor picked them up and brought them back.

Side note, my son showed his bike later that day and sold it for more money than he had bought it for.

In the end, it was a major inconvenience but it all worked out.

Bad news, the person or persons that stole the bikes never got arrested and are still at large, probably stealing more bikes.

I close with this because there is a thief who wants nothing more than to steal, kill, and destroy your life.

He studies your life.

He watches your patterns.

He knows your vulnerabilities.

He wouldn't attack you if you weren't valuable.

This thief that Jesus talks about has stolen so many years and chapters of our lives. In many cases, we bear the scars of years of hurt, shame, and abuse.

What I want you to know is that not only does God see you and love you, but He also wants to steal you back.

FULLY ALIVE

He wants to redeem what has been stolen. He wants to restore you to His original purpose.

As you walk out this journey, I won't tell you that it will be easy, but I will promise you that it will be worth it.

Don't let the thief have the final word. Take God at His.

> *"I have come that they may have*
> *life and have it to the full."*
> —John 10:10

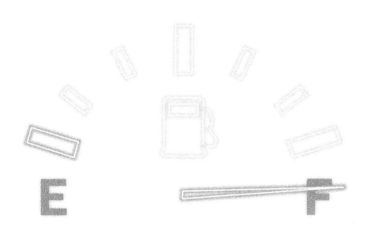